THE POWER OF THE POSITIVE

Achieve Fulfillment, Success and Happiness
Using Powerful, Positive Affirmations

COLLEEN ARCHER

Table of Contents

Introduction

Every day of our lives, we are telling ourselves stories. When you wake up in the morning and think about the day ahead, you are narrating the story of your day in advance. When you meet someone new and describe your daily life, talk about your past, or confide your hopes for the future, you are telling the bigger story of your life.

Now, you might think that whether that story is happy or sad, hopeful or despairing, bright or gloomy, has to do with what has happened to you. You might think that the story of your life is out of your hands, controlled by some dark forces conspiring to keep you unhappy, unfulfilled, and dissatisfied.

That's where you're wrong. You are the only one in charge of how you tell the story of your life. Haven't you met people who have experienced great tragedies or suffering in their lives, but who speak as though each day were a gift, or who are thankful for the hardships they've endured? These people have learned how to give their own stories a positive arc and a happy ending, and so can you. Just like the way you part your hair or the way you make soup, the story you tell yourself and the way that you think are habits. And these habits can be changed using affirmations.

Affirmations are short, positive

statements about you or your life. They might be as simple as, "I accept myself," or "I am successful in all that I do." These positive statements are a new way of telling your story, even if just to yourself. If you develop an affirmations practice that gets you to say these affirmations on a regular, frequent basis, you will be successful in changing your subconscious thought patterns. These subconscious thought patterns are like the narrator of your story. To change the story of your life, all you have to do is teach this narrator to speak in a new, more positive way.

Your inner narrator might already be starting his or her pessimistic monologue: "That's baloney. You will never be happy or satisfied. Change isn't that simple and, even if it were, you'd probably fail at it like you fail at everything. You don't even really deserve to be happy." Wouldn't it be nice to replace that narrator with one that spoke in a more positive way? One that spoke more like this: "Of course you will be happy and satisfied. You are successful at moving towards your goals and making positive change. You deserve all the best things in the world." Affirmations absolutely can teach you to speak to and about yourself in a radically accepting, positive way.

You might also be wondering how you ended up with such a negative self-image in the first place. It's not surprising, though. You have probably spent most of your life absorbing negative thoughts, because they are all around us. TV commercials work by telling us that we're inadequate, that we're not happy enough, not tidy enough, that we don't have enough stuff, that we aren't having enough fun. And TV commercials and other advertisements suggest that it is more *things* that will lead to greater happiness. By now, you have to know that that isn't true. But hearing constantly how inadequate you are has likely made you feel self-conscious and dissatisfied with your life, even though you already have all you need to make you happy.

Many of us have been told we aren't enough on a more intimate level, too. Partners, parents, other family members, friends, teachers, co-workers, bosses, all of these people are constantly making criticisms, directly or indirectly, that can become internalized. I know that I am my own worst critic, but I had to learn to become that way from somewhere outside myself. Whatever the source of your self-criticism and negative self-talk, you can learn to achieve real self-acceptance and a deep sense of satisfaction through replacing self-criticism with self-praise. After all, the external critical voices will always be there, reminding you any time you really do make a mistake. But only you can give yourself the praise, acceptance, and inner peace that you deserve.

If re-writing your life story to a more

positive version sounds like something you want to learn to do, you are in the right place. This book will teach you everything you need to know to get started on an affirmations practice that can develop into a lifelong change of your habits. Every ending can be happy, and even your story can be hopeful and bright. All you have to do is change the way you tell it.

How to Use This Book

This book will give you all the tools you need to develop a successful affirmations practice that will help you transform your life by transforming your thinking. It absolutely works to read this book straight through, but if you want to skip around, you should feel free. Below are some recommendations for different approaches to reading this book:

- If you want to learn more about what affirmations are and how they work before jumping into developing an affirmations practice, you will want to start reading this book from the beginning.
- If you are religious or have a meditation practice and are most interested in learning how to incorporate affirmations into your existing spiritual beliefs and practices, you might want to start with

"The Roots of Affirmations."

- If you are already know about the positive benefits of affirmations and want to get started with developing an affirmations practice right away, skip to "Traits of Successful Affirmations," and "Create Your Own Affirmations."
- If you have already learned about affirmations from another source, or if you have unsuccessfully tried to adopt an affirmations practice in the past, you are probably looking for new strategies to help you develop an affirmations practice that actually sticks. If this is the case, skip to "How to Make Your Affirmations Stick."
- If you are looking primarily for a list of pre-made affirmations to incorporate into an existing affirmations practice, you may want to begin with the "Affirmations Directory."

Many sections of this book contain a **Try It Now** exercise that will help you get started with using affirmations right away. This isn't one of those books that dangles all the useful information in front of you but holds it back until the end. You can start trying affirmations right away as you learn more about them. You can also skip past these exercises if you want to get more of an overview before beginning your affirmations practice. But remember: the only way to make positive change is to take action, so, if you can, give these exercises a try.

It might be useful for you to understand what each section of this book contains, if you need more help deciding where to begin:

- The first section of this book, "What Are Affirmations?" is designed to give you an overview of what affirmations are and what an affirmations practice is, with a little bit about how these powerful tools work.
- The second section, "The Roots of Affirmations," explores the relationship between affirmations and other religious and spiritual practices. This section can help you make connections between your affirmations practice and your other spiritual or religious beliefs. It also will show you that affirmations share deep spiritual roots with other religious beliefs and practices.
- The third section of this book, "The Benefits of Affirmations," focuses on exploring the benefits of affirmations and describes the ways that affirmations can work to transform your life.
- The fourth and fifth sections, "Traits of Successful Affirmations," and "Create Your Own Affirmations," are all about

the nuts and bolts of creating affirmations that will help you achieve your goals, conquer your fears, and develop positive self-esteem.

- The sixth section, "How to Make Your Affirmations Stick," provides a variety of strategies for developing an affirmations practice that will stick, using a variety of approaches.

- The final section, the "Affirmations Directory," is a list of affirmations geared towards particular topics. These lists can be used in conjunction with the affirmations you create on your own in the earlier section.

One of the suggestions in "How to Make Your Affirmations Stick" is to keep an affirmations journal where you keep lists of affirmations that appeal to you and where you write down any positive effects you experience from using affirmations. If this idea appeals to you, you may want to read this section right away, and start keeping a journal or taking notes while you read this book. You can also use the highlight or bookmark feature on your e-book reader to mark passages or affirmations that seem especially useful to you.

What are Affirmations?

This section will give you an overview of what affirmations are and what an affirmations practice looks like. First, you'll learn that affirmations are short, positive, present-tense statements about yourself, your life, and the world, that are meant to create positive change in your life. Next, you'll learn what an affirmations practice looks like. To truly gain the rewards of affirmations, you need to create a regular, focused practice of saying affirmations, so that their power will become internalized, and your negative thought processes will take a turn for the positive.

Definition

The American Heritage Dictionary explains that the noun "affirmation" means "Something declared to be true; a positive statement or judgment." In this way, any statement you make about yourself, or others, or the world, is an affirmation, something you are declaring to be true. So, for example, if you say "I am such an idiot," this is an affirmation. By saying it, you are claiming that it is the truth. If you say "Nothing good ever happens to me," you are claiming that this is the truth. On the other hand, if you say "I am a valuable person," you will be claiming the truth too, and in claiming it, you'll be on your way to making it true. If you say "The world is offering its richness to me," you will be claiming this other, more positive truth and impacting all your interactions with the world.

For the purpose of this book, you can think of an affirmation as a short statement that expresses a positive truth about the world. Affirmations can range from simple and broad, to more complex or focused. "I accept myself," is one simple, powerful affirmation that most of us could stand to incorporate into our lives. But an affirmation could also focus on a specific goal or task, like "I am a good daughter to my parents," or "The world is bringing me the answers I need about my health."

The power in affirmations is that the statements we make about ourselves and the world tend to become true. In fact, our thoughts about ourselves and the world are in many ways more important than the actual events that happen to us. I can think of a great example of this principle using some people I know.

Two of my friends were laid off from their jobs in the last year. Let's call them Nancy and Diane. Nancy, a generally pessimistic, negative-minded person, was laid off from her job at an accounting firm. She kept telling me about how useless this proved she was. "I'm never going to be able to find another job," she would say. "I'm never going to be able to adapt to a new workplace. I suck at computers. People never like me when they first meet me. It's hopeless." A year later, after several interviews, Nancy is still not working, and has dug herself into a deep hole of depression and anxiety in the meantime.

Diane was laid off from a similar position in an insurance office. Rather than see this situation as proof of her incompetence or inability, or as an opportunity to criticize herself, Diane used this opportunity to do some soul-searching. She told me, "I see this as an opportunity to expand my skills and pursue my passions. I am sure that there is something better out there for me." Diane took some cooking classes at the local library and decided to start the catering company she had always dreamed of. Now, a year later, her business is growing, and more importantly she is infinitely happier and knows that the future holds great things in store for her.

The power of affirmations is revealed in stories like these. Diane's positive view of herself helped her transform a bad situation into a good one, while Nancy's negative self-image made a bad situation worse. Both women had similar skills and were at similar points in their lives, but they told their stories in dramatically different ways. The same situation can yield drastically different outcomes, just based on the way you talk to yourself about it. Your life is a story and you are the narrator. How you choose to tell your story is up to you.

What Does an Affirmations Practice Look Like?

As defined in the previous section, affirmations are short statements that express a positive truth about yourself or the world. We are constantly saying affirmations to ourselves throughout the day, either out loud in conversations with others, or just internally in our own minds. However, for many of us, these affirmations are negative rather than positive.

To try to change that, you have to develop an affirmations practice. At first, you will learn to incorporate these statements into your life in a habit-forming way. You might decide to keep an affirmations journal, say affirmations every day in the morning or the evening, use technological cues for affirmations, or leave reminders around your house. The section "How to Make Your Affirmations Stick" outlines in detail a variety of methods for developing an affirmations practice. Saying affirmations on a regular basis is like practice for the new, positive thoughts that are going to take over your mind. Practicing these positive thought habits in a structured way will eventually transform the thoughts that happen when you're not even paying attention.

Have you ever tried to change or break a habit? If you have ever quit smoking, started an exercise routine, or stopped biting your nails, you know that at first you need to dedicate all your energy to forming this new routine, but eventually it becomes second nature. All of us have experienced this on some level. Say one of your co-workers gets married and changes her last name. The first few times you write or type her name, you probably wrote in her former maiden name. Maybe you actually sent an e-mail or wrote a check to her using this old name before you realized your mistake. After making that mistake, you probably thought to yourself, "Okay, next time I am going to remember to write Davis instead of Smith." It took some thought and effort for a few more tries, but eventually you started writing the right name without even thinking about it. You changed your habit.

Changing your negative thought patterns works the same way. After practicing forcing the positive thoughts into your internal and external voice, eventually your unconscious mind will start repeating those thoughts without any effort. Rather than thinking "I'm worthless and a loser," when you make a mistake, your mind will automatically say "I accept and forgive myself."

Try it Now: Let's try a simple affirmations exercise right away. Choose one of the affirmations from the following list and repeat it to yourself out loud three times right now.

- I accept and forgive myself.
- I am at peace in my body.
- I am successful in all that I do.
- I am powerful and in control of myself and my life.
- I draw love towards me in all that I do.
- I already have everything I need to be happy.
- The world is a peaceful place.
- I am stronger than I think.

Set a timer for an hour from now and say the same affirmation again. Then, write this affirmation out longhand and leave it in a place where you will see it and repeat it again before you go to bed. At the end of the day, reflect a little on whether you felt a difference each time you reminded yourself of your affirmation. Did your affirmation help you cope with stress? Did it help you feel more positive and focused? Did it keep you from feeling bad about something you've done?

To fully transform your mind, you will need to develop a regular habit of saying affirmations. If you are interested in incorporating that habit into your other spiritual practices, such as meditation or prayer, read on to the next section. If you are not interested in learning about the relationship of affirmations to these other spiritual practices, skip to the section "The Benefits of Affirmations."

The Roots of Affirmations

Affirmations are often associated with the New Age, spiritual, and self-help movements, but the concept of making positive statements to transform the world has roots in other belief systems. Affirmations are not unlike the Christian practice of prayer, although affirmations focus more on the self, while prayers may focus more on addressing a higher power. Affirmations are also similar to meditation practices. Both affirmations and meditation certainly share the same intended outcome of achieving a more positive mental state. If you happen to be a Christian or have a meditation practice, you can incorporate affirmations into your existing spiritual practice, or incorporate spiritual elements into your affirmations. But whatever your religious beliefs, you can use affirmations to transform your life.

Affirmations and Prayer

If you are Christian, Jewish, Muslim, or a member of one of many other religions, you are likely familiar with the concept of prayer. Prayers can take many forms, but many involve positive statements of faith, or positive statements about God or one's self. These kinds of prayers are similar to affirmations. Prayers tend to be addressed to or focused on a higher power, while affirmations tend to be more focused on the self, but there is a certain amount of overlap between these practices.

The Lord's Prayer, one of the most common Christian prayers, contains the line "Forgive us our sins for we ourselves forgive everyone who is indebted to us." This statement of forgiveness is indeed an affirmation. This prayer serves as a reminder that the speaker should be feeling forgiveness, whether or not he or she started out with that feeling. Just saying that you feel forgiveness is often enough to trigger you to feel actual forgiveness, whether for big things or small.

Another common prayer is known as the Serenity Prayer. The Serenity Prayer is a powerful prayer that has been around for almost a thousand years. Today, this prayer is often taught as part of Alcoholics Anonymous and other twelve-step programs. The prayer says, "God, grant me the serenity to accept the things I cannot change, the courage to change things I can, and the wisdom to know the difference." This idea of accepting what cannot be changed and transforming what can be is very similar to the idea of affirmations. Your affirmations should encourage you to embrace and accept yourself, while also helping you transform your life for the positive. If you are already someone who repeats this prayer, you are well aware of the power of affirmations. If you like this prayer, you might incorporate it into your affirmations practice.

You can also use religious texts as a source to generate positive affirmations for your life. You can take your favorite quotes from the Bible or another religious text that have to do with yourself, others, or the world, and adapt them into affirmations. Below is a list of some Bible verses that might be useful affirmations:

- I have been set free because I know the teachings of Jesus and obey them. (John 8:32)
- Although I have many trails and sorrows, I have peace in Jesus because He has overcome the world. (John 16:33)
- God loves me so much that His son died for me so that I can live eternally. (John 3:16)
- I will speak and listen to pleasant words; they are sweet to my soul and healing to my bones. (Proverbs 16:24)
- He sent forth his word and healed me and he rescued me from the grave. (Psalm 107:20)
- I make God my dwelling and my refuge. No harm will befall me; no disaster will come near. He commands his angels concerning me to guard me in all my ways. (Psalm 91:9-11)
- I called to Lord my God for help and He healed me. (Psalm 30:2)

- I worship the Lord and his blessing is on my food and water. He takes away sickness from me and gives me a full life span. (Exodus 23:25-26)

Using these Biblical statements as your affirmations will not only help you transform your life for the positive but also deepen your faith and relationship with your religion or spirituality. If these spiritual beliefs are important to you, these affirmations will be even more effective.

Try It Now: Spiritual beliefs can be incorporated into an affirmations practice in two main ways. First, if you are someone who prays regularly, you may simply want to incorporate more affirmations, meaning positive statements about yourself, into your prayer practice. You will learn more later in the book about how to create these affirmations. Second, if you want to develop a specifically spiritual affirmation practice, you can incorporate prayers from your belief system or affirmations drawn from religious texts into your affirmations practice. These affirmations can be used just as you would use any other affirmations and can be integrated into your affirmations practice along with more secular affirmations. This book will focus primarily on secular affirmations, but you can easily incorporate your own spiritual beliefs.

Affirmations and Meditation

Affirmations also share sacred roots with Buddhist practices, especially meditation. The cornerstone of Buddhism is the practice of meditation. During meditation, you learn to clear your mind of thoughts, helping you replace negative thought patterns with positive ones. Although the techniques are slightly different, an affirmations practice and meditation share the same goal of creating a more positive mindset.

Although meditation practices come from ancient belief systems like Buddhism and Hinduism, meditation has become popular for people of all faiths today. Meditation classes are offered at many community centers and schools throughout the country, and there is a wealth of meditation videos, CDs, and books available, many for free online. If you are interested, developing a meditation practice would be a great supplement to your affirmations practice.

The meditation practice perhaps most closely aligned with affirmations is Transcendental Meditation. This form of meditation was invented and popularized in the 1960s when popular figures like the band The

Beatles began practicing this form of meditation. Transcendental Meditation involves using sounds or mantras to stimulate a heightened spiritual state. Mantras are words that are supposed to contain spiritual, transformative power, much like affirmations. One of the most famous mantras from Transcendental Meditation is "Om mani padme hum." This mantra is difficult to translate from Sanskrit into English, but the words mean "Generosity," "Ethics," "Patience," "Diligence," "Renunciation," and "Wisdom." During meditation, you chant this mantra and reflect on its meaning, as a way to transform yourself into a better person.

Much like affirmations, Buddhist practices of meditation and mantra-chanting use the power of positive statements and thinking to transform the minds and lives of practitioners. If you already have a meditation practice, you can incorporate affirmations into that practice by choosing affirmations to serve as mantras. You can also begin or end a meditation session by repeating an affirmation to yourself. You could even record yourself reciting several affirmations and use it as a background track while you meditate.

> **Try it Now:** If you have never tried meditation, or you do not meditate regularly, but are interested in developing a meditation practice using affirmations,

you can try this exercise. Choose an affirmation that has to do with yourself and self-acceptance. A powerful affirmation for most of us is simply "I accept myself and forgive myself," but you could choose another if you wish. Sit in a quiet room with no possibility of distractions. This means you should silence your cell phone, tell your family to leave you alone, and be sure you have some un-interrupted time. You do not have to sit cross-legged or use any special materials. Simply sit in a comfortable position on a chair or on the floor with your eyes open or closed, whichever is more comfortable. Set a timer for ten minutes. Begin by saying the affirmation you have chosen out loud to yourself slowly five times. Then, sit in silence, and concentrate on your breathing. You should breathe in and out slowly through your nose. On your out breaths, think your affirmation. When your timer alerts you ten minutes has passed, say your affirmation out loud to yourself five more times.

If you would like to learn more about meditation, check out *How to Quiet Your Mind* by Marc Allen. Whether or not you think of it as meditation, an affirmations practice will help you develop a more trained, focused, and positive mind.

The Benefits of Affirmations

Affirmations can and will literally change your life. That might sound like a bold claim, but developing an affirmations practice will help you re-train your mind to think in a more positive, optimistic way. This change in thought patterns matters more than any change in your external life factors. If you change the way you think about your life, you will have changed your life, and you will invite more positive change to come in the future.

Developing an affirmations practice has four main benefits. The first is the main goal of affirmations: to change your thoughts from a negative, self-destructive pattern to a more positive, healthy, and happy cycle of thinking. In doing this, affirmations will also give you a second benefit: higher self-esteem. The third benefit of affirmations is that they help you focus your energies on your goals and intentions. The fourth benefit is that affirmations can help you accept events or aspects of your life that cannot be changed. All of these benefits combine to create an overall increase in your happiness and success. With a positive self-image and clear intentions, there will be nothing you can't do.

Positive Thinking and its Rewards

The entire purpose of developing an affirmations practice is to re-train your mind so that it no longer gets stuck in negative thought patterns, but instead dwells on the positive aspects of yourself and your life. Affirmations work not by asking you to **stop** thinking negative thoughts, but by asking you to **start** thinking positive thoughts that can replace those negative thoughts. This kind of positive thinking holds many benefits to your mind and body.

Think of your mind as being like an ocean, and you—your spirit or soul—are like a boat on that ocean. Negative thoughts are like rough water. Positive thoughts are like the wind in your sails. Negative thoughts come with no warning, forming sharp peaks and valleys that make your little boat toss and rock. Even if there are some positive thoughts that fill your sails with air, you are going to find yourself frequently tossed off course by the waves. You will have to spend most of your energy keeping your little boat afloat and above water, rather than using that energy to chart your course or search for land. If you can learn to still the waters, and blow more air into your sails, you will be able to spend that energy on your true pursuits. Affirmations can help you achieve this calm mind by training your mind to avoid negative thoughts and dwell on positive thoughts instead.

As if having a more peaceful, positive mental state isn't enough of its own reward, researchers from the Mayo Clinic have discovered that there are many health-related benefits to developing a more positive outlook. These benefits include:

- Living longer
- Lowering your risk of depression
- Being less likely to catch a common cold
- Reducing your risk of death from heart disease
- Being better able to cope with stress

Researchers say that positive thinking might explain these benefits in two ways. The first is that people with a more positive outlook might be better able to cope with stress. Stress is extremely harmful to the body, so experiencing less of it would have many added health benefits. Secondly, people with a more positive outlook might be more likely to lead healthier lives. More optimistic people might be those more likely to exercise regularly, eat healthfully, and avoid health risks like smoking cigarettes or drinking alcohol excessively.

Try it Now: Try an affirmation exercise for positive thinking right now. A powerful affirmation for developing a positive outlook on the world is simply

"The universe is leading me in the right direction." Say this affirmation out loud to yourself three times right now. Write this affirmation on a Post-it or a piece of paper and stick it in a place where you will see it several more times today, maybe next to your computer, on your mirror, or above your kitchen sink. Notice how much calmer and less worried you feel about your life and what's to come when you are practicing the belief that the world is working things out for the better.

An affirmations practice that helps you develop a more positive outlook will help you transform your mind and your body for the better. If you are skeptical, thinking that the world just plain **isn't** leading you in the right direction, remember that that outlook is just a habit. It might be a habit you have held onto for a long time, but that doesn't mean that habit can't be changed. An affirmations practice can be the first step towards making a habit out of believing in a more peaceful, positive outlook.

Improving Self Esteem and its Benefits

Affirmations help you develop a more positive outlook about the world, and also about yourself. If your first response to the idea of thinking positively about yourself is "No way," you're not alone. From a young age, most of us get messages that we are not good enough, whether from our parents, our teachers, or even from the TV. Magazines paper the newsstands telling us how to flatten, tighten, and straighten our never-good-enough bodies. TV shows display luxurious, immaculate homes that most of us could never hope to own. And various people in our lives have told us that we're not smart enough, not caring enough, not creative enough, and so on, until we've taken that message to be true.

This kind of outlook, while common, is extremely dangerous. According to the BBC Health, low self-esteem is linked to an increased risk of anxiety and depression. Even worse, low self-esteem often becomes part of a vicious cycle of actions that keep you trapped in a state of low self-esteem. When you think lowly of yourself and your abilities, you are less likely to do something that might actually improve your self-esteem or help you cope with depression or anxiety. Thinking about yourself as worthless will lead to depression, but thinking of yourself as worthless will keep you from seeking help to overcome the depression because you won't think of yourself as worth the energy. Having low self-esteem also makes it less likely you will engage in healthy, self-esteem building activities like exercising, eating right, and participating in nourishing social activities. When you think of yourself as worthless, you think of time spent taking care of yourself as unnecessary.

We can't do anything directly about the messages that have come to us from outside, but affirmations can help re-train the voice inside to stop repeating those nasty, self-limiting messages. Developing a healthy level of self-esteem has many benefits. According to the Mayo Clinic, increased self-esteem can lead to these positive effects:

- Better ability to assert your needs and ideas
- Increased confidence in your decisions
- Ability to form healthy relationships and avoid unhealthy relationships
- More realistic expectations of yourself and others
- Decrease in self-criticism and criticism of others
- Better resiliency and ability to cope with stress
- Decreased likelihood of feeling despair and guilt
- Less chance of developing mental health issues like eating disorders, addictions, depression, or anxiety

Try it Now: This book has two exercises in the "Create Your Own Affirmations" section that are designed to help boost your self-esteem, but you can try this small exercise right away. A simple, powerful affirmation for self-esteem is "I am a valuable person. I deserve happiness and success." Go stand in front of the mirror you look into most often, or the one you look into before you go out for the day. Look yourself in the eye and say this affirmation out loud to yourself three times. Don't shy away if this feels uncomfortable. It will take practice to fully un-learn the bad habit of low self-esteem. Next write this affirmation on a post-it note or scrap of paper and stick it to the mirror. Every time you look into this mirror, say the affirmation out loud, looking into your own eyes. After a few times of doing this, or a few days, you will start to feel more comfortable with the idea. Write down any other positive benefits you notice as a result of saying this affirmation.

Increased self-esteem is an important element you need to achieve your life goals. In order to accomplish what you desire, you have to believe both that the world is always working out for the best and that you are worthy of success and rewards. Affirmations that build up your self-esteem will give you permission to succeed be the best possible version of yourself.

Focusing on your Goals and Intentions

The primary goal of an affirmations practice is to transform your negative thoughts into positive thoughts, and give your self-esteem an infusion of positivity too. With all of that positive momentum brewing inside you, you will already be well on your way to a more successful life. But affirmations can also help you achieve some specific goals by helping you stay focused on what you want out of life.

Just the act of clarifying your goals in the process of creating affirmations can help you achieve your goals. Many of us have a sense of where we'd like our life to go, but we may not always be the best at creating a plan to make our dreams a reality. Creating affirmations based on your goals can help you by making large, abstract goals more manageable and concrete. For example, if you set a goal to "be healthier," you might not be sure when you've achieved that goal. But if you focus on a smaller, more achievable task like "eating six fruits or vegetables per day," you will be more likely to feel success. Affirmations can help you narrow down your goals and think about what positive steps you can take each day to bring you closer to happiness.

Affirmations can also serve as reminders

to help you stay focused on your goals. Many of us like to dream big about the day when we will have the perfect job, the most beautiful home, and a healthy body. But the only way to get to that dream life is to make small, positive steps in the right direction every day. It might not seem like much is happening on a daily basis to make that dream a reality, but that might be because you aren't actively focusing on your goals. Every time you miss a networking opportunity, or let clutter pile up, or grab a fast food hamburger, it is likely because you have lost sight of your goals and the small steps that will help you achieve them. Reminding yourself every day of what you hope to achieve will help you make the right small choices to lead to the big pay-off.

Some people also believe that positive thinking can manifest positive change in the world outside of yourself. This idea, called the law of attraction, was popularized most recently in the movie and book *The Secret.* The law of attraction is the idea that thinking positive thoughts will create positive outcomes in the world. So, if you have a job interview and spend the whole interview thinking and believing that you will get the job, the law of attraction states that you will in fact get the job. Of course it's hard to say whether you got the job because of a metaphysical force rather than the improved self-esteem you projected because you were thinking confidently. Regardless, keeping focused on your goals and dreams is the only way to make them come true.

> **Try It Now:** The "Create Your Own Affirmations" section of this book will explain in detail the process of creating affirmations based on your goals, but if you want to get started right away, you can try this exercise. Think of a goal you would like to achieve before the end of the day today. Maybe your goal is to spend some relaxation time reading a magazine after work, or to go to the gym, or to re-organize your desk. It's best if this is something you have been meaning to do but haven't quite gotten to. Rather than beating yourself up about not getting to this task yet, your affirmation should assert that you are the kind of person who always gets this task done. For the example of reading a magazine, your affirmation might be, "I make time to relax." For the example of going to the gym, it might be, "I make healthy choices." For the example of re-organizing your desk, you might say, "I am organized and competent." Say this affirmation out loud to yourself three times. See if that helps you get motivated to achieve your small goal. If you have to wait until later to complete your task,

repeat your affirmation throughout the day. Since this task has likely already been weighing on your mind, simply try to replace the thought of "I should do that later" with your affirmation.

Affirmations can help you achieve both long-term goals and short-term goals by helping you stay focused on those goals and prioritize your life to make the right choices. A successful affirmations practice will help you come one step closer to your goals every day.

Achieving Peace Through Acceptance

Although the previous sections have detailed the ways that developing an affirmations practice can help you create positive change in your life, affirmations can also help you accept and make peace with the parts of your life that cannot be changed. This acceptance comes hand-in-hand with developing a more positive self-image and nurturing increased self-esteem.

Positive thinking certainly has many extraordinary benefits, but it also has its limits. To illustrate this, let's think about trying to land a new job. You need to focus on thinking positively during the entire process of applying for the job. You want to think highly of yourself as you write your cover letter, stressing your strengths and downplaying any shortcomings. If called in for an interview, you have to appear confident and dress in a way that is flattering for your body. Positive thinking can help you come across as a great candidate for a job, by making sure your shoulders are straight and you are acting like a person who is already hired. This kind of confidence often leads to success. Having great self-esteem and thinking like you are a great candidate for the job puts you in the best possible position to get hired.

However, positive thinking alone can't prevent someone more qualified than you from applying for the job, or keep the hiring manager from giving the job to his less-qualified nephew. Positive thinking can't necessarily help you if the train you take to the interview is delayed by an hour, making you terribly late. Sometimes, bad things are going to happen, or things aren't going to turn out as you had envisioned.

While it might sound like this is admitting that affirmations don't always work, it is actually a case for using affirmations even more. Affirmations can help you turn what looks like a negative into a positive. If you don't get the job, you can use affirmations to help you think of this as a new opportunity for growth. You could see missing out on this job as a chance to work even harder to develop skills and experience that would make you a competitive candidate for an even better job. More positive thinking and self-confidence can help you nail the next job interview and land the job.

Try It Now: Think about something that has recently disappointed you. Maybe you have just applied for but didn't get a new job. Maybe someone in your life let you down. Maybe you made a mistake at work or failed to be there for a friend. Think of something small, but something that has been nagging at you, and something that has already happened so you can't do anything to change. Now, you are going to create an affirmation that directly counters the disappoint you feel.

If that disappointment is directed at yourself, for something that you did "wrong," your affirmation could be as simple as "I accept myself." It could also be something more specific that says the direct opposite of the criticism you are making of yourself. If you recently let someone down and are feeling like a bad friend, your affirmation could be "I am a good friend." If you made a mistake at work, your affirmation could be "I am a capable and competent employee [or teacher, manager, etc.]"

If your disappointment is focused more

on things outside of your control, your affirmation could again be a simple one like "The world offers me many opportunities." It could also be an assertion of your worth, even if you have recently faced rejection. If you did not get hired for a new job, you could say "I am skilled and capable at what I do." If someone close to you let you down, you could say "I am loved and respected."

Once you have chosen your affirmation, say it out loud to yourself three times. Then, set a timer to remind you to say the affirmation again every hour for the next three hours. See if you can feel more positively about your disappointment by the end of the day.

When something happens that is outside of your control, it is a waste of your valuable energy to spend time fretting, stressing, or wishing things were otherwise. Instead, using affirmations and positive thinking, you can continue to channel your energy towards your goals and maintain peace and composure throughout the ups and downs of life.

Traits of Successful Affirmations

Now that you've learned about all the positive benefits of affirmations, you are ready to start creating your own affirmations. Successful affirmations all share a few common traits. Affirmations should be relatively short. They are usually one sentence, but can occasionally be two. Affirmations should also always be positive. You are likely already a pro at negative affirmations; now you should focus on crafting positive affirmations. Your affirmations should also always be in the present tense. This section will delve into further detail on each of these aspects. Once you know what your affirmations should look like, you can move on to the next section, which explains how to craft affirmations based on your specific needs.

Keep it Brief

Since your affirmations will be things you repeat to yourself over and over, you want them to be brief and memorable. Although longer affirmation-like statements might be useful to you, you will be able to get more power out of a shorter affirmation.

Furthermore, keeping your affirmations short keeps them focused and positive. Simply saying "I honor and respect myself" is actually enough. If you try to make it longer, you may just be distracting from your focus. If you don't keep yourself to a short, simple sentence, you may end up with an affirmation like this: "I honor and respect myself in all of the choices that I make throughout my life, especially when it comes to my relationships." Although the sentiment here is great, it is a lot harder for your mind to process. Also, the first, shorter affirmation is more powerful because it can apply more broadly to your life and your attitude about yourself.

Also, sometimes longer affirmations are a sneaky way of allowing negative thoughts into your affirmation. For example, you might write a longer affirmation like this: "Although I have made many mistakes and do not always act the right way, I honor and respect myself." That's not much of an affirmation at all! By including the negative thought in the longer affirmation, you give those thoughts power.

When you are creating your own affirmations, **try to keep the affirmation to one, short sentence**. Trim out any unnecessary fluff and focus on the most important attitude you want to convey. You should be able to write most affirmations out by hand in one or two lines of notebook paper. If you type your affirmation, it should contain no more than 75 characters.

Accentuate the Positive

Although your typical thought patterns may veer toward the negative, your affirmations must be completely positive. The point of affirmations is to re-train your mind to achieve more positive thinking, so it is absolutely essential that your affirmations contain no negative terms.

As mentioned in the previous section, your affirmations should not contain any "although" or "but" statements that distract from the positive message. You should not say "Although I struggle with honesty, I am open and truthful in all that I do." Instead, just say "I am open and truthful in all that I do." Instead of saying, "My body is healthy, whole, and loved, but I wish it were lighter," just say "My body is healthy, whole, and loved." Those negative statements, however slight, will detract from the positive power of your affirmation.

Even if your affirmation is about changing a habit, working towards a goal, or transforming some aspect of your life, that change should be framed positively. If you want to create an affirmation about quitting smoking, you should do so in a way that emphasizes the new, positive things you will be taking on in place of smoking. For example, an affirmation that says "I do not desire to smoke" is not as powerful as an affirmation that says "I breathe clean, fresh air." If you are creating affirmations for weight loss, an affirmation that says "I will not give in to temptation" is not as powerful as an affirmation that says "I am strong and in control of myself and my life." Do you see how the first affirmations are giving the negative thoughts power, while the seconds are replacing the negative with a positive thought?

Here is a list of some **negative** words your affirmations should never include:

- Not
- No
- Never
- Can't
- Don't
- Won't
- Shouldn't
- But
- Although
- Instead
- Despite

Here are some positive words that many of your affirmations might include:

- I am
- Yes
- Always
- Can
- Do

- Accept
- All

If on your first attempt, an affirmation comes out with some negative words, don't feel bad. It takes a lot of hard work to un-learn those negative thought patterns. And don't get rid of that affirmation. Simply revise it so that it is a positive affirmation with no negative terms.

Talk About Now

So far you've learned how to make your affirmations short and positive, but the third important aspect of your affirmations is that they are written in the present tense. A little grammar lesson can help you figure this step out.

Each of your affirmations is going to contain a verb. Remember that a verb is a word that expresses action or state of being. Many affirmations use a form of the verb "to be" such as "am," "is," and "are." We use different forms of the same verb to express different tenses, or different positions in time. Affirmations should always be written in the present tense, to indicate that they are happening in the present. Here are some examples to show you affirmations written in the present versus the past versus the future tense.

<u>Past</u>: My body **used to be** healthy, strong,

and powerful.

<u>Future</u>: My body **will be** healthy, strong, and powerful.

<u>Present</u>: My body **is** healthy, strong, and powerful.

<u>Past</u>: I **was** open to receiving the gifts of the world.

<u>Future</u>: I **will be** open to receiving the gifts of the world.

<u>Present</u>: I **am** open to receiving the gifts of the world.

<u>Past</u>: I **used to be** a good parent.

<u>Future</u>: I **will be** a better parent.

<u>Present</u>: I **am** a good parent.

The only difference in each version is the verb tense. Notice how the present tense versions of the affirmations make it clear that this affirmation is something happening right now. Affirmations focused on the past are a form of negative affirmation. Don't those affirmations sound like missed opportunities? Your affirmations should not dwell on past mistakes, or even past successes, but should create positivity in the present. Since the goal of affirmations is to transform your life immediately, starting the moment you say an affirmation, it is crucial to say affirmations in the present and not the past.

Affirmations written in the future tense are also not as powerful as affirmations written in the present. Many of us make plans to make positive change in our lives but never succeed at achieving that change. That's because many of us think about those changes as happening in the future, instead of thinking of them happening in the present. Instead of thinking "I will eat better," just think "I eat well."

For a change to happen in our lives, the first thing that has to change is our thinking. Keep your affirmations in the present tense and you'll be well on your way to making that positive change a reality.

Create Your Own Affirmations

When you are first getting started with affirmations, it is okay to stick with pre-written affirmations, like those offered in the "Affirmations Directory" in this book. But to fully transform your thinking, you will want to create your own, personalized affirmations. These affirmations will work best for you because they address your own specific needs. Not sure what those needs are? That's okay, too. This section will help you identify your goals, fears, and weaknesses, and start transforming yourself and your life through positive affirmations.

And remember, the affirmations you create in this section should follow the basic guidelines outlined in the previous section. **Remember, all affirmations should be brief, positive, and present tense.**

Turning Goals into Affirmations

There are two main types of goals that affirmations can help you achieve: long-term goals and short-term goals. You may have a clear sense of what those goals are, but if you don't, here is an exercise that can help you figure them out.

Take out a few pieces of paper, or use some pages from your affirmation journal. On the first page, write a description of what you want your life to look like one year from now. Be as specific as possible. When I have done this exercise with high school seniors, they sometimes write things like "I'll be in college and have a girlfriend." I always encourage them to get even more specific, with a description like, "I'll be at the end of my first year at Penn State as a biology major. I will have earned all As, played intramural basketball, and joined the chess club. I will have a girlfriend who is kind, smart, and funny." Do you see the difference? One version is just a statement of facts, while the other is a **description** of a future life. Make your description as specific as possible and focus on the big picture aspects and the little picture details. Maybe you want to buy a house or find a new job, but maybe you also want to plant a garden, adopt a dog, and re-connect with an old friend. Your description should also include details about what kind of person you will be, and how you will **feel** one year from now. Probably, you will imagine yourself as happy and at peace, and that's an important part of your vision.

Now, repeat this activity but think about what you want your life to look like five years from now, and then ten years from now. Think about what you want to have achieved and what kind of person you want to be. Again, make your descriptions as vivid and specific as possible.

Think of yourself as a character in a novel or a movie, and describe that character's life. Dream big, but also be realistic. The odds that you could become a famous musician are pretty slim, but the odds that you could learn to play the guitar, start a band, and play local concerts are pretty high.

Once you have written these descriptions, break them down into concrete, specific goals, and try to write those goals in order of when you want them to happen. My sample list for one year from now might look like this:

- Lose ten pounds
- Build a better relationship with my mom
- Learn to play the guitar
- Travel to California

Long-term goals like this don't happen overnight, and most of them are things I couldn't procrastinate on if I wanted to make sure that they happened in the next year. So, I need to break those goals down into smaller activities I can do every day, like these:

- Eat more fruits and vegetables
- Call my mom once a week
- Start taking guitar lessons and carve out time to practice
- Save money and stockpile sick days from work

See how much more achievable my goals sound already? These are little things I can do every day, and I can craft affirmations that will support me on my way. The affirmations I will create to achieve those goals might look like this:

- I honor my body and health by choosing healthy foods.
- I am a caring and thoughtful daughter.
- I am talented and my talents are worth pursuing.
- I attract wealth, and I will see the world.

If I make it part of my daily routine to repeat those affirmations to myself, not only will I have a calmer, more positive thought process, but I will also remind myself of my goals and intentions. Keeping these goals at the forefront of my mind will help me make the right choices to make those dreams a reality.

You should repeat this step for your five-year and ten-year visions, especially paying attention to goals that seem to overlap. Those are the goals that must be most important to you, and so those are the first things you should choose to focus on as affirmations.

Long-term goals can only be achieved by changing short-term actions, and short-term actions can only be changed by changing the present moment. We have to think about the future to identify our goals, but the only way to make those goals happen is to bring them into the present through affirmations.

Keeping Fear from Inter-Fearing

Sometimes what stops us from achieving our goals is more than just not recognizing or identifying those goals. Sometimes what stops us from achieving our goals is our fears. If you want to develop a better relationship with your partner, but you fear the vulnerability that comes with being open and intimate, it might not be enough to set a goal. First you might have to address your fears. Affirmations can be an effective counter to these kinds of fears that suffocate us and hold us back, because affirmations can turn these fears into strengths.

Overcoming a fear is kind of like breaking a habit, as fears have a way of making themselves habitual. Although your fears come from a genuine, often spontaneous, place deep within you, the behavior patterns driven by those fears can become bad habits that you need to break. Fears are, after all, a kind of negative thinking. "I am afraid to do this" is another way of saying "I can't." Affirmations can help you learn to say "I can."

You might already know what fears are holding you back in your life, but, if you don't, your first step will be to identify those fears. To do this, return to the goals you outlined in the previous section. Most likely, you have attempted to achieve some of these goals previously, but have not been successful for one reason or another. Start to think about why and make a list. What fears have blocked your path in trying to achieve these or other goals? What fears hold you back from doing what you want to do?

Sometimes someone who is close to you, like a partner, friend, sibling, or parent, might be able to help you identify your fears. If you feel comfortable, try asking someone what things they notice you shying away from, or what fears you may express consciously or unconsciously. Thinking about your fears can be difficult, and sometimes emotional, but don't beat yourself up over these fears and the ways they may have held you back. Everyone struggles against their fears. The important thing is that you are making steps to overcome them.

Once you have identified your fears, you need to create affirmations that counter those fears directly. Here is a list of some common fears people have, and sample affirmations that work to take away the power from those fears.

If you like...	Possible Affirmations
Your sense of humor	I bring humor to any situation. I know how to take things in stride. I have a great sense of humor.

The support you give others	I am a caring friend [or family member]. I am always there for my loved ones. I am generous and caring.
Your creative abilities	I have many creative gifts. My talents are valuable. I am proud of my creative accomplishments.
Your smile	I have a warm and caring smile. I enjoy spreading warmth and cheer. I bring joy to others.

Your fears and affirmations might look a little different from those in this list, but you want to pin down your fears and then create affirmations that work to counter them. Think of these affirmations as the kinds of things a parent would say to a child. If a child says he is scared of the monster under the bed, the parent will say "There is no monster under the bed." The same is true even for bigger fears. If a child is scared that a parent will fall sick, the parent will say "I am healthy and well," even if it is of course a possibility the parent will fall ill. Think of your affirmations as coming from this same kind of place of self-care and self-assurance.

Painter Georgia O'Keeffe once said, "I've been absolutely terrified every moment of my life and I've never let it keep me from doing a single thing that I wanted to do." You are going to take the same approach. If you begin by re-training your thoughts so that your fears hold less power than the positive affirmations about them, you will be able to move past your fears and towards a more successful, powerful, and accomplished version of yourself.

Affirmations for Self-Esteem 1: Praising Your Strengths

In addition to helping you achieve your goals and confront your fears, affirmations can help you improve your self-esteem. Having low self-esteem is one of the biggest factors that holds people back from achieving success, so improving your self-esteem will also help you achieve your goals.

The first way to create affirmations to boost your self-esteem is to create affirmations that focus on the positive aspects of yourself. Although you might often find yourself focusing only on your faults, you can undoubtedly admit that there are certain things you are good at or are proud of yourself for having done. These points of pride can easily be transformed into affirmations. These kinds of affirmations work by providing you positive reinforcement for the good you have done, which can help you worry less about mistakes you might have made or shortcomings you may have.

To create affirmations focused on your positive traits or achievements, first you need to brainstorm what those are. Start by making a list of things you like about yourself. This might be things like your sense of humor, the support you give to others, your creative abilities, or even just your smile. Try to come up with at least one example of what you value about yourself from each aspect of your life, from your personal life to your work life to your inner life. Then create an affirmation about these traits. Your affirmations might look something like these:

If you like...	Possible Affirmations
Your sense of humor	I bring humor to any situation. I know how to take things in stride. I have a great sense of humor.
The support you give others	I am a caring friend [or family member]. I am always there for my loved ones. I am generous and caring.
Your creative abilities	I have many creative gifts. My talents are valuable. I am proud of my creative accomplishments.

	I have a warm and caring smile.
Your smile	I enjoy spreading warmth and cheer.
	I bring joy to others.

These affirmations of self-praise are very powerful affirmations that you can say every day. Although you may still struggle with negative thoughts about yourself, an issue we'll discuss in the next section, these affirmations can at least help you give yourself credit for your strengths.

Affirmations for Self Esteem 2: Accepting Your Flaws

The second way to create affirmations to boost your self-esteem is to focus on forgiving yourself and accepting yourself for past mistakes. Most of us devote too much energy each day to kicking ourselves for the things we do wrong. You might give yourself a hard time about something small or in your recent past, like not calling back a friend last week or being unkind to a grocery store clerk this morning. But you probably also have regrets about larger events in your more distant past, like treating a loved one badly or missing out on a big opportunity.

You can create affirmations that will help

you counter these feelings of regret and shame. This will free up space in your mind to help you focus on acting positively in the future. If you snapped at the grocery store clerk this morning and feel bad about it, the most important thing you can do is move towards acting more kindly in the future. If you hurt a loved one through your actions in the past, the best thing you can do is not repeat that mistake. Holding on to a negative image of yourself as a person who acts unkindly or carelessly will only make you more likely to make the same mistakes again. If you replace that negative self-image, however, with a positive one, you will be able to change your actions in the present and live with fewer regrets.

One of the most powerful affirmations to help you stop regretting mistakes or criticizing yourself for your past actions is a simple one. Try saying "I accept myself and forgive myself in the past, present, and future." This affirmation emphasizes not only forgiveness for your past mistakes, but also acceptance of your present and future failures and shortcomings. We all make mistakes sometimes; what is most important is that you acknowledge them, accept them, and move on.

You can also create more specific affirmations designed to replace negative thoughts you have about yourself. Sometimes it may be enough to simply assert something positive about yourself, as explained in the previous unit. But to experience true self-esteem, you will also want to directly address the negative thoughts you have about yourself.

First, think about what aspects of yourself you find yourself criticizing most. What parts of yourself do you find yourself thinking about changing most often? Also think about things you experience lingering regret, guilt, or shame about. While compiling this list might feel like an unpleasant task, I promise it will help you move past these feelings. The first step, though, is identifying the roots of those feelings. A sample list might look something like this:

- I wish I were more outgoing.
- I always leave things until the last minute and then have to rush.
- I regret having treated my sister badly in the past.
- I wish that I had tried harder in school.

Next, you have to create affirmations that state the opposite of what you usually believe to be true about yourself. You have to give yourself permission to forgive yourself for your past mistakes or shortcomings, and use them to create your better, present self. Sample affirmations for the above list might look like this:

- I am a friendly person and people like me.

- I respect my commitments and take them seriously.
- I am a loving, caring sister.
- I try hard in all that I do.

Although you might be saying to yourself that the above statements aren't true, these affirmations will eventually help silence that nagging, negative voice. And if you repeat these affirmations often enough, they will also make themselves true. You will be less likely to do the things you dislike about yourself if you see yourself in a more positive light. Letting go of the past and silencing that inner critic will allow you to truly flourish.

How to Make Your Affirmations Stick

In order to truly make positive change in your life, you have to commit yourself to that change. If you want to make the goals and dreams your affirmations are focused on a reality, you have to start using those affirmations every single day. This is the part where most of us fail. How many times have you said to yourself, "I'm going to start exercising every day," or "I'm going to stop eating so much fast food," only to fall back on old habits within a week.

At this point in this book, you may be thinking "I'm going to start saying my affirmations every day," but wondering how you will make that true. Studies have shown that to form a new habit, you have to do the new task every day for twenty-one days. So to establish a new, positive thought pattern using affirmations, you have to dedicate yourself to saying affirmations every day for about three weeks. This section will show you how.

Since everyone has different methods that work for them for establishing a habit, I've offered you a variety of possible strategies to get you in the habit of saying affirmations. Try whichever methods most appeal to you, or have worked for you in the past, and try several in combination to see which reminders are most effective.

What is most important is that you choose at least one of these methods and commit to sticking to it for the twenty-one days it will take to make affirmations an integrated part of your life. If you miss a day, and fall back into old, negative habits, don't beat yourself up about it. The great thing about affirmations is that you can pick up right where you left off. Just turn things around by saying "I forgive myself and accept myself," and be back on your way to a more positive outlook.

Affirmation Journaling

One of the best ways to make affirmations a part of your daily life is to keep an affirmations journal. Writing down your affirmations is another way to give them power, just liking saying them out loud or thinking them to yourself. Your affirmation journal can also be a space to write new affirmations, or journal your progress with making positive changes.

You can use a simple spiral-bound notebook to use for your affirmations journal, or you can choose a more embellished journal from a bookstore if you prefer. You want to choose a journal that is sturdy and comfortable to write in. You may want to choose a small journal that you can tuck in your bag or briefcase, so you can have it with you throughout your day. You may also want to use a journal that stays on your night table as a bedside reminder of your affirmation goals.

You should divide your affirmations journal into two sections: one for writing your affirmations for each day and tracking your progress through diary entries, and one for keeping lists of the affirmations you use, for easy reference. Some journals may come split into sections that would work well for this, but you can also simply work both forwards and backwards through the journal, keeping your daily entries in the front, and your running lists in the back.

Each day, in the daily entries section, you should write down the affirmation or affirmations you have chosen to focus on that day. You should write each affirmation out at least once, but writing the affirmation out several times is also effective. Did you ever notice how you are more likely to remember something when you write it down? The same is true for affirmations. Taking the time to hand-write your affirmations each day can put your affirmations at the forefront of your mind. Also, in the few minutes you spend writing down your affirmations, you are completely focused on them, just as you are when you are saying your affirmations out loud or to yourself.

You also may want to write a few notes about the affirmations you are using, and any positive changes you may have noticed as a result of using them. While this may not seem useful to you at the time you write it down, it will be fun and insightful to look back over your journal entries and note the positive progress you've made towards changing your thoughts. These journal entries also might help you identify topics for new affirmations, if you realize certain doubts or insecurities keep re-appearing. It is important, however, to try and keep the daily entries in your affirmations as positive as the affirmations themselves. If you are feeling negative, try to keep that attitude out of the pages of your affirmation journal. This journal should be a positive space to make your affirmations come true.

You should also keep lists of the affirmations you use or want to use in the future. You may want to break these affirmation lists into categories, using some or all of these suggested headings:

- Affirmations for Goals
- Affirmations against Fears
- Affirmations for Self-Esteem
- Affirmations for Health and Healing
- Affirmations for Love and Relationships
- Affirmations for Happiness
- Affirmations for Peace and Acceptance
- Affirmations for Relieving Stress
- Affirmations for Overcoming Addictions
- Spiritual Affirmations

You can also make up your own category headings or develop your own organizational methods; these are just suggestions. You can dedicate several pages in the back of your affirmations journal, or in a separate section, to keeping these running lists.

If you are more technologically-oriented, you may prefer to type your journal on your computer or into a journaling website. If you do this, though, keep in mind that physically writing your affirmations out is more effective than simply typing them. Try to supplement your digital journal with writing your affirmations out by hand, even if you simply do this on scrap paper near your computer.

Morning Affirmations

Have you ever noticed how things that happen first thing in the morning have a way of sticking with you for the whole day? If you wake up spooked by a nightmare, or wake up to find bad news waiting in your inbox, you may feel like the whole day got started on the wrong foot. Even something small, like spilling your first cup of coffee, can seem to create a negative cloud that hangs over the whole day.

The opposite is equally true, however, so saying affirmations first thing in the morning can be a great way to start your day. Saying affirmations in the morning is also a good way to make affirmations part of a routine. Most of us are creatures of habit when it comes to waking up. You probably go about your morning routine, from making coffee, to eating breakfast, to brushing your teeth, without giving it much thought. Incorporating saying affirmations into that morning routine can make sure that your affirmations will become part of a habit that sticks.

Saying affirmations first thing in the morning is also a way to give your affirmations more power. If the first thing you do each day is say an affirmation, your affirmations will be more likely to manifest themselves throughout the day. If you begin your day with an affirmation like "I accept and value myself," you are more likely to carry that attitude with you throughout the day. After saying that affirmation, when you look at yourself in the mirror while getting ready, you'll be more likely to think a positive thought about yourself than a negative one. And this pattern will continue throughout the day. Starting the day with an affirmation will make that affirmation come true more easily.

Another benefit to saying affirmations in the morning is that affirmations help you focus on your goals and intentions. If you are using affirmations to try to make new, positive habits, or work towards a particular goal, you are more likely to be successful if you begin the day by setting that intention. For example, you might begin the day with an affirmation like "I attract wealth and prosperity with all I do." This will help you focus your activities and energies throughout the day, reminding you of your priorities. You might be more likely to skip that morning splurge on breakfast or more likely to spend time on entrepreneurial pursuits later in the afternoon if you establish the goal of attracting wealth first thing in the morning.

> **Try It Now:** Think about where in your morning routine you have time to dedicate five or ten minutes to your affirmations practice. This might be right away when you get out of bed, or it might be after you're dressed and ready but before you walk out the door. Just make sure that it is a time you will give priority to and not skip past if you are running late.

To establish a habit of saying affirmations every morning, you might need to set up some kind of reminder. You can simply leave a note for yourself on your alarm clock, in the bathroom near your toothbrush, or on the coffeemaker. Think about what you look at every morning and place a note there reminding you of your affirmations. You could also set up a repeating calendar alert on your cell phone or computer that will send you a text message or e-mail reminding you to think of your affirmations at a certain point each morning.

If you are someone who usually starts the day in a state of stress or panic, it might be especially useful to carve out time for affirmations in the morning. On the other hand, if adding affirmations into your morning routine would create more stress than it would dispel, don't force yourself to try this method. There are many other ways to incorporate affirmations into your life, so try the time and place that feels most suitable to you.

Nightly Affirmations

The end of the day is an equally useful time to establish a habit of saying affirmations. Just like morning affirmations, nightly affirmations can be a way to reflect on your life day-to-day and establish intentions, this time for the following day. You can try saying affirmations both in the morning and at night, you can do one or the other, or you can try some other methods for incorporating affirmations into your life.

At night, you can't change anything about the day that has just happened, but you can use the nighttime to reflect on the successes or failures that day and practice affirmations for acceptance. If you are saying affirmations both morning and nightly, you can use the nighttime to reflect on whether you felt your affirmations working throughout the day or not. You can consider if you should be saying your affirmations more often if you think you lost sight of the intentions set by your affirmations during the day. Remember, of course, that change occurs gradually, so don't use nighttime reflection as an opportunity to be overly self-critical. You are on the road to positive change just by taking the time to reflect.

Nightly affirmations have the added benefit of helping you fall asleep and calm yourself at the end of a long day. If you are someone prone to difficulty sleeping, as I am, you may be familiar with the endless stream of mostly negative self-talk that can take over the mind while it is lying still. Those negative thoughts can be easily pushed away by reciting affirmations out loud or in your head. Affirmations can help you accept and feel calm about whatever has happened in your day, and this feeling of calm can help you drift off to sleep more easily, and maybe even have more positive dreams.

Try It Now: Evening or nighttime affirmations can happen at any point near the end of the day. What is most important is that you choose a part of your nighttime routine where you can work in affirmations as part of a daily practice. If there are certain TV shows you watch every evening, you can carve out time before or after they start. You can even try turning the TV on mute during commercial breaks and saying affirmations during these breaks. Many people like to use the time right before sleep, while sitting in bed, as a time to say affirmations and reflect on the day. Choose whatever time sounds most appealing to you, and that sounds like a time when you will be able to commit to practicing your affirmations.

To establish a habit of saying nighttime affirmations, you may want to set up reminders for yourself, similar to the reminders suggested for morning affirmations. Think about what your nightly routine usually looks like and find a place to leave a note reminding you to use your affirmations. This might be on the drawer where you keep your pajamas, in the bathroom near your toothbrush, or on the corner of your TV. If you are using an affirmations journal, you might remember to use it if you leave it on your bedside table.

If incorporating affirmations into your evening routine sounds more stressful than peaceful, it is perfectly okay to develop your affirmations practice at a different time of day. If you usually just feel like dropping off to sleep when you get home at night, the evening might not be the best time for you to say affirmations. If that's the case, you might find saying affirmations in the morning more appealing, or you might try a different method for saying affirmations.

Affirmation Cues

Establishing a routine to say your affirmations is important. However, if you work an irregular schedule, or don't consistently have time in the mornings or evenings, you may want to try using "affirmation cues." The idea of affirmation cues is borrowed from Thich Nhat Hanh's book about mindfulness, *Peace is Every Step.* Thich Nhat Hanh recommends choosing a sound that you hear often throughout the day and using it as a cue for mindfulness. The same idea can be used to develop cues to remind you to say or think an affirmation throughout the day.

This is a particularly useful method because it incorporates affirmations into your life at intervals throughout the day, not just in the morning or at night. Since the goal of an affirmations practice is to transform the thought processes taking place constantly in your mind, using affirmations frequently throughout the day will bring you closer to this goal. You might especially like this method if your schedule is irregular, or if you find it difficult to carve out time at the beginning or the end of the day. This method can also be used in conjunction with morning or nightly affirmations as a way to spread your affirmation practice out throughout the day. This is particularly important if it seems like you forget to keep your affirmations in mind in the middle of the day.

The great thing about this method is that once you successfully associate a certain cue with an affirmation, the affirmations will become almost automatic. The brain works by forging connections between associated memories. This is why seeing a toy from your childhood might make you feel happy and free, or why the smell of applesauce always makes you think of your grandmother, or why hearing a certain song can take you back to being a teenager. Associating a positive affirmation with a certain sound that occurs often in your life will form a similar brain connection. This automatic brain connection will keep your affirmations repeating in your mind, with hardly any conscious effort!

The automatic nature of affirmation cues means that your affirmations practice will still be working, even if you slip up in other areas. If you miss your morning affirmations for a few days, but your affirmation cues are in place, you will still be thinking positive thoughts throughout your day.

> **Try It Now:** First, you have to choose a cue. Think about a sound you hear frequently throughout your day. For me, it might be a noisy bus passing outside my window. For you, it might be the sound of receiving a text message or e-mail, a neighbor's dog barking, or a squeaky printer at work. It can even be good if this is a sound that usually causes you irritation, because that means you usually notice it. You could also establish an affirmation cue with a particular sight, such as a person walking past your office, a car driving past your house, or light reflecting off of a mirror. You just want to choose something that occurs several times through the course of the day and that will stand out to you.

> The next time you hear that sound or see that sight, even if it initially causes you annoyance or irritation, use it as a reminder to say an affirmation. If you are also doing morning or nightly affirmations, use the same affirmation

you recited that morning or the previous night. If you have time, you can flip through your affirmation journal and look for an affirmation you might need. If you've been having a stressful day at work, you might need an affirmation that assures you of your competence and calm. If you've been feeling regret over a mistake you made that morning, you might want to say an affirmation for self-forgiveness and acceptance. If you have been distracted from your goals, you might want to say an affirmation re-setting your intentions for the day. If you can't think of a particular affirmation, or don't want to take a break from what you are working on, simply say a basic positive affirmation like "I accept and honor myself."

For the first week or so of using affirmation cues, you may also want to create a reminder system so that you remember to say your affirmations. For this, you can leave a note in your office at work, on your car dashboard, or even on something related to your cue like your cell phone or computer. Eventually, though, you will form a habit of saying an affirmation every time you hear your cue.

If you say an affirmation every time you hear your chosen affirmation cue, you will be on your way to establishing a more positive attitude throughout your day. When left alone, the mind will tend to return to its old, stagnant thought patterns. To get your mind moving in a positive direction more often, you have to stir it up with affirmations repeated all day long.

Mirror Affirmations

Think about where in your house your most viciously negative self-talk happens. If you're like many people, that place may be in front of a mirror. "Look at those thighs!" "When did I get so fat?" "I wish I had a flatter stomach." Sound familiar?

If you're someone who hates looking in the mirror because you know you will start thinking negative thoughts at yourself, or if you're someone who stands in front of the mirror every day picking apart your flaws, the mirror may make a great ground zero for re-shaping those attitudes through affirmations. To replace those negative thoughts with positive ones, you have to establish a new habit of saying affirmations in front of the mirror.

Saying positive things about yourself while looking in the mirror, although this may at first be uncomfortable, is one of the most effective ways to use affirmations. Saying affirmations while looking in the mirror has the added benefit of allowing you to make eye contact with yourself. Although this can be uncomfortable at first, it is ultimately a more powerful way to make an affirmation stick. Eye contact can be a very powerful component of communication with another person, and, strange as it may seem, the same is true when communication with yourself.

If you usually find yourself criticizing yourself while standing in front of the mirror, you should first focus on creating some specific affirmations that counter the criticisms you make. These affirmations can be as simple as "I love my body" or "I love _____" about a specific part of your body. Even if you are trying to change your body by losing weight or getting in shape, you should still treat your body with respect and kindness. Focus on the positive aspects of those activities by saying affirmations like, "I am healthy and strong," or "I make the right choices for my health."

> **Try It Now:** Think about which mirror in your house you stand in front of most. Stand directly in front of this mirror, look yourself straight in the eye, and say a positive affirmation. Try "I am a valuable being deserving of happiness and joy," or "I am healthy, beautiful, and whole." Did

you feel how powerful it was to say that to yourself?

To make mirror affirmations a part of your daily habit and routine, try hanging a reminder on the walls around your mirror, or even on the mirror itself. A sticky note right in your line of sight will remind you to change your negative self-talk to positive affirmations.

If you are having a difficult time saying affirmations while at the mirror, try hanging the full text of your affirmations on the walls around your mirror. This way, even if you struggle with changing an ingrained habit of negative self-talk while at the mirror, you will absorb the text of your affirmations and start to make positive change.

While affirmations about health and the body might be the most appropriate to use for mirror affirmations, you can incorporate any kinds of affirmations into a mirror affirmation practice. Mirror affirmations can also be combined with the types of affirmations outlined in the previous sections. Mirror affirmations can be done each morning or each night, like any other morning or nightly affirmation. Or, you can think of the mirror as an affirmation cue, with looking at your own reflection as a cue to say a positive affirmation about yourself.

If you don't find yourself looking into the mirror much, or if you already think positive thoughts about yourself when doing so, you may not find mirror affirmations particularly useful, so feel free to disregard this method in favor of others.

Technology for Affirmations

Many of us are spending more and more time plugged into digital devices of one kind of another. Although being constantly plugged in to technology can have its downsides, technology can also be used as a positive tool to supplement an affirmations practice. If you want to get high-tech with your affirmations, there are a wealth of ways to use your digital devices as reminders.

If you have a cell phone, whether it's a smartphone or not, you probably have a calendar or alarm feature. On most phones, you can set a recurring alarm or create a recurring calendar event to remind you to say an affirmation once a day, or even several times a day. Many people use this same kind of feature as a reminder to take medications that must be taken at the same time each day. Think of affirmations the same way, as something you need to remember to do in order to help yourself heal and grow. This is especially important in those first three weeks when you are trying to make affirmations a habit that sticks.

At the computer, you can do something similar with a digital or online calendar. These calendars can usually be configured to send you reminders via a pop-up window or e-mail. Some, like Google Calendar, can even send you a text message, too, so no matter where you are, you will remember to say your affirmations. If you frequently use a chat program or e-mail client that sends pop-up notifications or uses sound alerts, you could also use those pop-ups as affirmation cues. I know that I frequently lose track of time and lose focus on my purpose while at the computer, so if that happens to you, too, you might want to incorporate affirmations that establish your intentions into your computer use.

You might also want to add the text of your affirmations themselves, or a reminder to say them, somewhere on your computer or phone. You could type an affirmation into your screensaver, desktop background, phone banner, or in any other place that allows you to add text to your digital device. One of my former bosses used to have floating text that said "I love my job" as her desktop screensaver. Whether or not she felt that way when she walked into work every day, it seemed to become true by the time she sat down at her desk. She set herself up to say a positive affirmation every time she came to work or came back to her desk, no matter how stressed or frustrated she might have been by the rest of her day.

Of course if you are not that savvy with technology, or if you just don't spend much time with your computer or phone during the day, it can be just as effective to leave yourself notes or use other methods to make affirmations a habit. But if you spend a lot of time in your day staring at screens, you may want to find a way to incorporate your affirmations into your digital life.

__Affirmations Directory__

Although hopefully you will create some of your own affirmations using the methods explained earlier in the book, this directory is here to provide you with some affirmations to use as a jumping off point, or to use as a supplement for your self-created affirmations. These affirmations are divided by topic or purpose, with some affirmations appearing in multiple lists if they apply to multiple purposes.

To choose which affirmations to add to your affirmations journal and your affirmation practice, start by identifying which purpose you'd like an affirmation for. Then, read the list of possible affirmations out loud, taking note of any that seem particularly resonant. Some phrases might roll off of your tongue more easily or apply more directly to the problem you wish to address. If you're not sure, start with the first affirmation on each list one day, and try the second the next. Sometimes it takes actually trying an affirmation out to determine if it is worth using for you.

Remember, though, that the best affirmations will be those you create especially for yourself, those that address your own specific goals and fears, so do take the time to complete the exercises in the "Create Your Own Affirmations" section.

Affirmations for Health and Healing

- My body is healthy and strong.

- My body is always moving towards health and wellness.

- My body is my home and I treat it with love.

- I am at peace in my body.

- I am full of energy and life.

- My body is healthy, whole, and loved.

- I am healthy, beautiful, and whole.

- I make the right choices for my health.

- I love _____. (Insert specific part of body.)

- I love and cherish my body.

Affirmations for Prosperity

- The world is offering its richness to me.

- The universe is leading me in the right direction.

- I am successful in all that I do.

- I am worthy of success and happiness.

- I am on the path towards success and prosperity.

- The world is overflowing with opportunities.

- I attract wealth and abundance.

- My life is leading me towards success.

- I welcome success into my life.

- Success is my destiny.

Affirmations for Love and Relationships

- I am a good daughter (son, mother, father, aunt, uncle, niece, nephew, etc.).

- I am loved and protected.

- I am open to love that is coming towards me.

- I am honest and open in my relationships.

- I am happy in all my relationships.

- I draw love towards me in all that I do.

- I act with love towards all around me.

- My partner loves me the way that I am.

- I welcome love into my life.

- I deserve love.

Affirmations for Self Esteem

- I honor and respect myself.
- I accept myself and forgive myself.
- I am a valuable person and I deserve happiness and success.
- I am strong and resilient.
- I am powerful and in control of myself and my life.
- I am a good person and I deserve respect.
- My life is meaningful.
- I am confident and capable.
- I believe in myself.
- I make the best possible choices for myself and my life.

Affirmations for Happiness

- I deserve happiness and success.
- I am happy and joyful.

- The world brings me many joyful gifts.

- I already have everything I need to be happy.

- Happiness is abundant in my life.

- The world offers me happiness each day.

- Happiness is a choice I make each day.

- Happiness is my destiny.

- I attract happiness and joy with all that I do.

- I can always find happiness.

Affirmations for Peace and Acceptance

- The universe is leading me in the right direction.

- I am all the company that I need.

- I accept myself and forgive myself.

- I am at peace with the world and myself.

- I am open to receiving the gifts of the world.

- The world is a peaceful place.

- I accept whatever the world offers me.

- I accept the actions of those around me.

- Peace is always available to me.

- My body is made to be peaceful and calm.

Affirmations for Relieving Stress

- I feel calmness radiating through me.
- I am in control of myself and my life.
- I am capable of handling whatever comes my way.
- The world gives me only what I can handle.
- I am moving towards happiness and peace.
- Stress is temporary.
- Calm is always possible in my mind.
- Good news is always coming my way.
- Stress breeds strength.
- I am stronger than I think.

Affirmations for Overcoming Addictions

- I am free from cravings.
- I am strong and capable of resisting temptation.
- I am making important steps towards success.
- I choose health every day.

- I deserve full health and wellness.
- I enjoy breathing clean, fresh air.
- I enjoy healthful foods.
- My body is healthy and strong.
- I am in control of my health and my life.
- Health is a choice.

<u>Conclusion</u>

Now that you have read through this book, you should have learned all the basics you need to get started with an affirmations practice of your own. This affirmations practice will have many positive benefits, such as helping you think more positively, improve your self-esteem, focus on your goals and intentions, and achieve peace through acceptance. All these positive benefits will combine to help you lead a more successful, happy, and fulfilling life.

Now that you have the power to create your own affirmations, you can have a dynamic affirmations practice that adjusts to meet your needs. Remember that your affirmations should be short, positive, and present-tense. You have the tools to create affirmations that work directly to support your goals, conquer your fears, and boost your self-esteem. These three kinds of affirmations, perhaps in conjunction with other affirmations chosen from the "Affirmations Directory" or that incorporate your spiritual beliefs, will help you transform your mind and your life.

You also have the tools to put your affirmations practice in action. Remember that you want to stick with your plan for at least three weeks to get your affirmations practice to stick. Eventually, though, you won't have to pay any conscious thought at all to your affirmations, as the positive thoughts will have become fully absorbed into your unconscious mind.

Affirmations are a powerful tool that you can use throughout your life. You can start by using affirmations to focus on some short-term goals, or to address a crisis of self-esteem, but you can later use them for a different purpose, maybe to fight a fear or break an old habit. Whatever your current goals or needs, affirmations help you transform your life by transforming your mind. A mind that is focused on the positive and the present will allow you to become the best person you can become.

Remember that your life is a story and you are the narrator. If you choose to tell a positive story, that story will become true. Start telling yourself the story you deserve, the story you want to be true, and watch it become your new, happy reality.

**Visit
EmpowermentNation.com
to view other fantastic books,
sign up for book alerts, giveaways,
and updates!**

Made in the USA
Columbia, SC
18 July 2019